D1450744

WORLD'S GREATEST ATHLETES

ICE KINGS

By Ellen Labrecque

The **Child's World**
www.childsworld.com

Published in the United States of America by The Child's World®
P.O. Box 326 • Chanhassen, MN 55317-0326
800-599-READ • www.childsworld.com

ACKNOWLEDGMENTS

The Child's World®: Mary Berendes, Publishing Director

Produced by Shoreline Publishing Group LLC
President / Editorial Director: James Buckley, Jr.
Designer: Tom Carling, carlingdesign.com
Assistant Editors: Jim Gigliotti, Ellen Labrecque

Photo Credits
Cover: Corbis.
Interior: AP/Wide World: 3, 7, 8, 13, 14; Corbis: 27; Getty Images: 1, 5
(2), 11, 15, 17, 18, 20, 23, 24, 25.

LIBRARY OF CONGRESS
CATALOGING-IN-PUBLICATION DATA

Labrecque, Ellen.
  Ice kings / by Ellen Labrecque.
    p. cm. — (The world's greatest athletes)
  Includes bibliographical references and index.
  ISBN-13: 978-1-59296-789-6 (library bound : alk. paper)
  ISBN-10: 1-59296-789-2 (library bound : alk. paper)
  1. Hockey players—Biography—Juvenile literature. 2. Crosby,
Sidney, 1987——Juvenile literature. 3. Ovechkin, Alexander, 1985——
Juvenile literature. I. Title.
  GV848.5.A1L33 2007

CONTENTS

Hail Hockey's Newest Heroes!

SIDNEY CROSBY, AGE 18, RACES TOWARD HIS opponents' net. The Pittsburgh Penguins center chases down the puck and shoots before the opposing goalie can react. *Goal!*

Sidney slams himself into the glass behind the net in excitement. The NHL rookie star has scored his first pro goal. The fans at Pittsburgh's first home game in October of 2005 explode in applause.

The same month, rookie Alexander Ovechkin, age 20, didn't just score his first NHL goal—he scored two in his first home game as a left wing for the Washington Capitals.

Fans everywhere said, "Finally!" The National Hockey League was back on the ice for the 2005–06 season. The league had been shut down the previous season because of a **lockout**. Owners and players could not agree on a new contract, and the NHL became the first major pro sports league to miss a full season. Once play started in July 2005, league owners worried: Would hockey fans come back to the game?

Enter Crosby and Ovechkin. Crosby was the Number 1 pick in the 2005 draft. He is called the "Next One" because he scores and passes in the style of Wayne Gretzky, the NHL's all-time leading scorer, who was called the "Great One." Ovechkin was the first pick the year before. He can **stickhandle** smoothly through traffic and score often. He can also dish out some . bruising **checks**.

These two rookies are so sensational, they not only gave hockey fans reasons to come back, but also to smile again.

Alexander Ovechkin went from being a star in Russia to the NHL.

Sidney Crosby was destined for stardom from an early age.

CHAPTER 1

Growing Up Crosby

SIDNEY CROSBY WAS BORN IN COLE HARBOUR, Nova Scotia, Canada on August 7, 1987. He started skating at age three in his family's basement. His father, Troy, painted the floor white with a red line and a blue line and installed a net so it would look like an ice-hockey rink. Sidney and his dad played together all the time. Troy was formerly a hockey goalie who was drafted by the Montreal Canadiens in the 12th round of the 1984 NHL Draft. But, by the time Sidney was nine, the kid's slap shots were too tough for his dad to stop.

"He was killing me," Troy told *Sports Illustrated*. "I told him, 'You don't need a goalie, just shoot at the net.'"

Sidney wasn't just beating his dad in hockey.

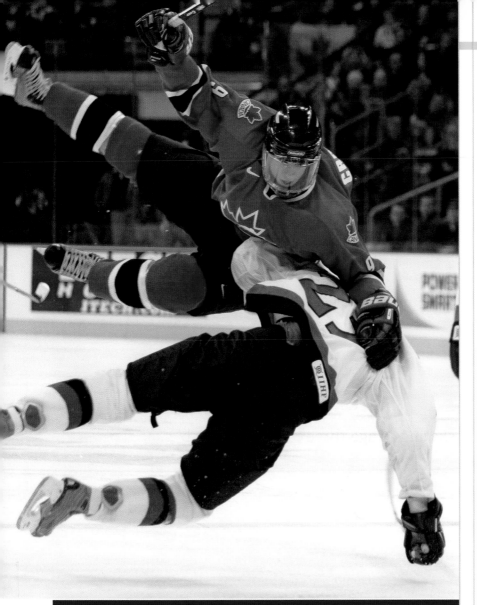

Hockey can be tough! Here's Sidney Crosby sent flying after taking a hard hit. Crosby combines tough play with great skills.

He was dominating the kids around him, too. At age 6, Sidney played in leagues with kids many years older. At age 14, he played in a league of 17 and 18 year olds and scored 106 goals in 81 games. The word was out on Sidney. It was time to move up.

In 2002, when Sidney was just 15, he moved to Fairbault, Minnesota, to play hockey for the Shattuck-St. Mary's School. The school is known for its dominant hockey program. Sidney scored 72

Playing in Canada's junior leagues, Sidney continued to score in bunches. The A on his jersey stands for alternate captain.

goals in 57 games in the 2002–03 season. If hockey fans and scouts didn't know about Sidney's skills before, they certainly did now. Sidney's play even caught the eye of the great Wayne Gretzky. In the summer of 2003, Wayne was asked if there was a young player who might one day break some of his 61 NHL scoring records. Wayne responded: "Yes, Sidney Crosby. He's dynamite."

Sidney left the Shattuck-St. Mary's School after one season to play for Rimouski Oceanic in the Quebec Major Junior Hockey League (QMJHL). QMJHL is one of the top junior leagues in all of North America. In Sidney's first season with Oceanic, he finished with a league-leading 135 points (54 goals, 81 **assists**) in 59 games. His **stellar** play quickly made him a fan favorite. The season before Sidney's arrival, Rimouski played in front of half-filled arenas. With Sidney as their star, games were played in front of standing-room-only crowds. "The Next One," though, was careful not to let this fame go to his head.

"I realize a lot of guys have been tagged with that 'next great player' thing," Sidney said. "Some have gone on to be great players, some have fallen. I don't want to be one of the guys who disappears."

Seven-time MVP Wayne "The Great One" Gretzky set just about every NHL career scoring record, including most points, most goals, and most assists.

Sidney only got better during his second season with Rimouski in 2004–05. He led the league in scoring again with 66 goals and 102 assists in 62 games. He also led his team to the finals of the Memorial Cup, which is junior hockey's version of the Stanley Cup.

In the meantime, Sidney was also excelling on the international stage. In 2003, at age 16, he was the only player under age 18 invited to join the Canadian Junior Hockey Team. He helped Canada win a silver medal at the 2004 World Junior Championships, recording five points during the tournament. At the

Young Sidney Crosby

▶ Sidney was born on August 8, 1987 (8/7/87). This is why his NHL number is, of course, 87.

▶ Sidney has had a personal trainer since he was age 13. During the summer leading up to the 2005 NHL draft, he spent his mornings doing sprints and free weights, and finishing up resting in the sauna.

▶ At age 7, Sidney was already so good at hockey, he was interviewed by a newspaper reporter.

NHL, here I come. After being picked by the Penguins, Sidney pulled on his first NHL hockey sweater for this photo.

2005 World Junior Championships, Canada captured the gold medal and Sidney finished with nine points.

Sidney was now ready for the big time. On July 30, 2005, the Pittsburgh Penguins selected Sidney as the Number 1 overall pick in the NHL Draft.

It was time for the Next One to take the next big step.

CHAPTER 2

Crosby Lives Up to the Hype

THE NHL WAS AS EXCITED TO HAVE SIDNEY PLAY in its league as he was as excited to be there. The season prior to the 2005 draft had been cancelled. Fans were angry. They missed watching hockey and rooting for their favorite players. League owners hoped Sidney, his skills, and his friendly personality would bring fans back to the game again.

"I realize people are looking for a [reason] to be interested in the game," Sidney told *Sports Illustrated for Kids* prior to the 2005–06 season. "It's a challenge for me, but I have to take things one step at a time."

Sidney played his first pro game against the New Jersey Devils on October 5, 2005. Although he did not score a goal in the 5–1 loss, he registered the assist. Three days later, in a 7–6 loss to the Boston Bruins,

Sidney couldn't have asked for a better teacher than Penguins' owner and former superstar player Mario Lemieux (left).

Sidney made his first goal. Mario Lemieux, the owner of the Pittsburgh Penguins and a former legendary NHL player himself who retired in January 2006, knew only more good things were to come for his team's future star.

"He's a great young player," said Lemieux. "I think he's going to create a lot of excitement around the league, around hockey, and especially in Pittsburgh."

As the 2005–06 season progressed, Sidney continued to show off his skills. At 5' 10", 180 pounds, Sidney could take hard checks with the best of them. He also saw passing lanes so well, it seemed like he had X-ray vision.

"Sid the Kid" also proved to be a determined scorer. Sidney finished the season with 39 goals (tied for 12th in the NHL) and 63 assists (7th). After just one season as a pro, he already had proved to be one of the league's best.

Far more important than past individual success, Sidney's focus now is to make the Penguins' team better. In 2005–06, Pittsburgh finished the season with the second-worst record in the league (22 wins, 46 losses, and 14 overtime losses). The Next One is still confident he will eventually turn the Penguins back into Stanley Cup winners. Pittsburgh previously won the Cup in 1991 and 1992. But as this NHL star said previously, he just plans to do things one step— or one puck—at a time.

In His Own Words

Sidney Crosby, on dealing with the pressure of becoming the NHL's next great player, as told to *Sports Illustrated*:

"Greatness isn't decided at 18. You can't say a player's good until he's played 10, 15 years in the league. Great players are the ones consistent year after year, the ones who win championships."

CHAPTER 3

Growing Up Ovechkin

TWO YEARS BEFORE SIDNEY CROSBY WAS BORN IN Canada in 1987, another future hockey star arrived. Alexander Ovechkin was born on September 17, 1985 in Moscow, Russia. Alexander was born with exceptional athletic **genes**. His mother, Tatiana, was an Olympic basketball player. She won a gold medal for the Soviet Union in the 1976 and the 1980 Summer Games. Alexander's father, Mikhail, was a top professional soccer player. Alexander, though, loved the sport of hockey from the beginning. His mother says that she took Alexander to a toy store when he was just two years old. Alexander toddled over to the toy hockey sticks and helmets and would not let go. "We have a picture with him as a toddler holding a hockey stick," Tatiana said.

Alexander spent his youth playing all kinds of sports—from basketball to soccer. But at age 7, he enrolled in the Dynamo Moscow sports school for hockey. The school allowed him to devote all of his free time, outside of schoolwork, to playing his favorite sport.

Tragedy struck Alexander and his family when he was just 10 years old. His older brother, Sergei, then 25, died in a car accident. Sergei had been a

Alexander first rose to fame while playing—and scoring— in Russia's professional league.

role model for Alexander and had encouraged his younger brother to pursue his hockey dreams. When Sergei died, Alexander was devastated, but knew his parents were just as crushed. Instead of thinking about his own pain, Alexander reached out to his mom and dad and tried to comfort them.

"One day during one of his hockey games," his mother said, "He looked up at the stands where I was sitting. He saw my eyes were full of tears and he ran up to me and told me, 'Mama, don't cry.'"

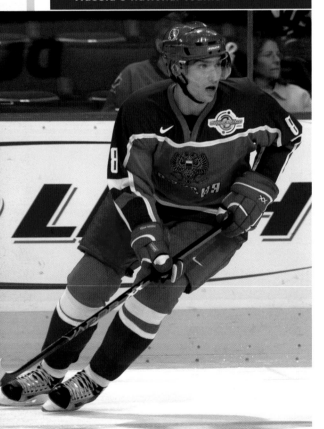

By 2002, Alexander was a big part of Russia's national teams.

Alexander began to use his brother's death as fuel to generate success. He knew that is what Sergei would have wanted. Alexander's first goal was to work his way up to play in the Russian Superleague, which is thought of as the second best hockey league in the world. His ultimate goal, though, was to play in the best league—the NHL. Alexander continued to play and excel for Dynamo Moscow throughout

Young Alexander Ovechkin

▶ Alexander wears the number 8 because that was his mother's number. His mother, Tatiana, was a two-time Olympic gold medalist for the Soviet Union women's basketball team (1976, 1980). He would sometimes wear his mother's medals while he was growing up, pretending he had won them.

▶ Alexander's favorite player growing up was Soviet Union Olympic ice hockey great Alexander Maltsev. Maltsev won gold in the 1972 and 1976 Olympics and a silver medal in 1980.

▶ The Florida Panthers tried to select Alexander with a pick in the 2003 NHL draft. But Alexander missed the age-eligibility deadline by two days. He had to wait to be drafted Number 1 in 2004, at the age of 18, by the Washington Capitals.

his youth. By age 16, he reached his first **objective**. He made his debut in the Superleague in 2001. He scored two goals and two assists in 21 games. The next season, Alexander only got better. He scored eight goals and seven assists in 40 games. In the 2003–04 season, at age 18, Alexander scored 13 goals and made 10 assists in 53 games. He won the league award for Best Left Wing. It was finally time for Alexander to join the best league in the world. The NHL was calling.

CHAPTER 4

To the NHL and Beyond

ON JUNE 26, 2004, ALEXANDER WAS TAKEN NUMBER 1 overall in the NHL Draft by the Washington Capitals. He was only the second Russian ever drafted in the Number 1 spot. The Capitals loved Alexander's speed and creativity. The 6' 2", 212-pound winger did anything to score—whether it meant making a **deke** to fool a defender or simply bulldozing a defender down. What Capitals owner Ted Leonsis liked best about Alexander wasn't just the way he scored goals.

"I've learned that hockey is really a team game," Leonsis said. "This kid is a team player who makes those around him better."

Washington couldn't wait to get its future star on the ice. But, unfortunately, the Capitals did have to wait: The NHL shut down for the 2004–05 season because of the lockout. Alexander went back to Russia and led Dynamo Moscow to a league championship.

The NHL settled its disputes in time for the 2005–06 season. From his first NHL game, Alexander dazzled opponents. Through the first 65 games of the season, he scored 43 goals (second in the league). He also had 41 assists (tied for 31st). Alexander not only scored a lot of goals as a rookie, he also scored important ones. In the first 37 games of the season, six of his goals were the first goals of the game for the Capitals, nine of his goals gave his team the lead, and two were game winners.

"Is Alexander the most talented guy I've ever played with?" Washington goalie Olaf Kolzig said to *Sports Illustrated*. "Yes. That's because he uses his talent to the fullest all the time."

Alexander impressed teammates with his skills on the ice and his attitude away from the rink. Coming from Russia, he took on a new language and a new **culture** when he came to play in the United States. But instead of shying away from his new experiences, Alexander embraced them. He worked

What were the disputes in the NHL lockout? It was complicated, but basically, the owners felt that they were losing money by paying players too much.

The power of Alexander's shot is shown in this photo, which captures how much his stick bends when he shoots.

at learning English by watching TV news. During down time, Alexander hung out and played cards with his North American teammates.

"When I came here, I was little bit nervous," Alexander told *Sports Illustrated*. "New team. New language. But now it's like I'm here five years."

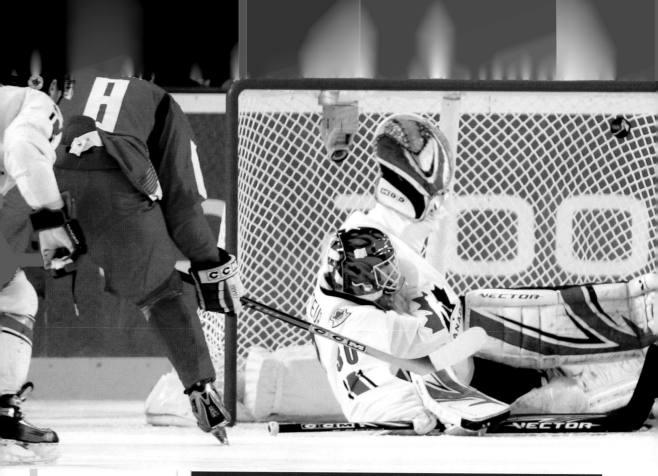

He shoots . . . he scores! Playing for the Russian national team, Alexander (8) fires a shot past a Team Canada goalie.

Even though Alexander fit in well in Washington, he was still a Russian at heart. Early in the NHL season, he wrote the word "Russia" on a whiteboard in the team locker room before every game. He also loved to play for his home country in international competition. He played in three World Junior Championships and helped Russia win the gold medal in 2003. In 2005, he led his country in goals (seven) and was named the tournament's best forward.

Russia won the silver medal. At the 2005 World Championships, Alexander led his team in goals and Russia won the bronze medal. Next up was a chance to play for Russia at the 2006 Winter Olympics.

"Representing your country is the biggest thrill," Alexander said before the Games began. "At the Olympics, I will be glad to represent my country."

Russia lost to the Czech Republic in the bronze medal game, 3–0. Alexander still scored a team-high five goals in Olympic play. No matter where he plays and in what uniform, Alexander finds the net.

In His Own Words

Alexander Ovechkin, on scoring:

▶ *"It's no secret that I love to score. But if I score a couple of goals and we lose, it takes away from the satisfaction from scoring."*

On why he walked away from stardom and certain riches in his native Russia to play in North America:

▶ *"The NHL was my dream when I was very young. I love the NHL. I wanted to play with these superstar players."*

CHAPTER 5

What's Next for the Ice Kings?

AFTER THE OLYMPICS, OVECHKIN WENT BACK
to play for the Capitals—and continued to dominate.
He finished the 2005–06 season with 52 goals (tied
for third in the NHL) and 53 assists (tied for 20th).
But, just as his Russian team lost in the Olympics, his
NHL team struggled, too. The Capitals finished with
the fourth-worst record in the league (29–41–12).

Alexander and the Capitals faced fellow
superstar rookie Sidney Crosby and the Pittsburgh
Penguins four times. They both played exceptionally
well. Pittsburgh won three of the four games. Crosby
scored three goals and made five assists during the
four match-ups, while Alexander had three goals
and three assists. After the regular season ended,
both players were named finalists for the NHL's

The two hottest rookies in the NHL—Crosby (left) and Ovechkin—met four times during the 2005-06 season.

Calder Memorial Trophy, awarded each season to the league's top rookie. After the season, Alexander was announced as the winner, while Crosby finished second in the voting. Crosby became the youngest player in league history to score 100 points, and he led all rookies with 63 assists.

No matter how these young stars do against each other, they both have the same goal in mind: to turn their teams—the Penguins for Sidney and the Capitals for Alexander—into winning franchises.

"Sometimes [Sidney] is the best. Sometimes I'm best," Alexander said. "But we must play how we can. We must play for the team. Each year the Capitals will have a chance to get stronger," Alexander continued. "So let's watch and see what happens."

That is exactly what hockey fans plan to do: Watch Ovechkin and Crosby become two of the best NHL players ever. But most importantly, fans will watch these young stars try to turn their teams into Stanley Cup champions. The outstanding careers of Sidney Crosby and Alexander Ovechkin have only begun to unfold.

A Good Teammate

As he accepted the Calder Trophy as top rookie in June 2006, Alexander reflected on how he had achieved so much success so quickly. "My coaches trust me a lot and they told me if I have a chance to do something, do it and don't be afraid to make some mistakes because you have great partners. Learn from your mistakes and play the way you can."

Career Statistics

Sidney Crosby

BORN: August 7, 1987   **BIRTHPLACE:** Cole Harbour, Nova Scotia, Canada
HEIGHT: 5-11   **WEIGHT:** 193
POSITION: Center   **SHOOTS:** Left

Season	GP	G	A	P	+/-	PIM	PP	SH	GW	GT	Shots	Pct.
2005-06	81	39	63	102	−1	110	16	0	5	0	278	14.0
Career	81	39	63	102	−1	110	16	0	5	0	278	14.0

Alexander Ovechkin

BORN: September 17, 1985   **BIRTHPLACE:** Moscow, Russia
HEIGHT: 6-2   **WEIGHT:** 216
POSITION: Left Wing   **SHOOTS:** Right

Season	GP	G	A	P	+/-	PIM	PP	SH	GW	GT	Shots	Pct.
2005-06	81	52	54	106	2	52	21	3	5	0	425	12.2
Career	81	52	54	106	2	52	21	3	5	0	425	12.2

LEGEND: GP: games played; G: goals; A: assists; P: points (goals plus assists); +/−: plus/minus rating (a figure arrived at by totaling the number of even strength and shorthanded goals a player's team scores while he is on the ice compared to the number the team allows while he is on the ice); PIM: penalties in minutes; PP: power-play goals; SH: shorthanded goals; GW: game-winning goals; GT: game-tying goals; Shots: shots on goal; Pct.: shooting percentage.

GLOSSARY

assists   in hockey, passes that lead directly to goals

checks   a hard body-to-body hit in hockey

culture   the customs or way of living of a particular group of people or country (in this case the United States)

deke   to fake out or fool

genes   chemicals in a body that transmit information about how that body will form and grow

lockout   in sports, a way for labor disputes to be resolved, in this case by preventing players from playing or practicing

objective   when used as a noun (as it is in this instance), it means an aim or a goal

stellar   outstanding, very good

stickhandle   move the puck around the ice by using the stick to control it

BOOKS

Hockey: How to Play Like the Pros
By Sean Rossiter and Paul Carson
Vancouver, British Columbia, Canada: Greystone Books, 2004.
This book is for youngsters who are interested not only in
reading about ice hockey, but also in learning how to play
this exciting sport.

Sidney Crosby: A Hockey Story
By Paul Arseneault
Halifax, Nova Scotia, Canada: Nimbus Publishing, 2005.
Another look at the Penguins' young center in a book for
young adults.

Sports Great Wayne Gretzky
By Ken Rappoport
Berkeley Heights, New Jersey: Enslow Publishers, 1996.
While Sidney Crosby and Alexander Ovechkin are two of
hockey's rising young stars, you can read all about perhaps
the greatest player ever in this book.

WEB SITES

Visit our home page for lots of links about Alexander Ovechkin,
Sidney Crosby, and the NHL: www.childsworld.com/links

Note to Parents, Teachers, and Librarians: We routinely check our Web links to
make sure they're safe, active sites—so encourage your readers to check them out!

INDEX

ABOUT THE AUTHOR

Ellen Labrecque is a former senior editor at *Sports Illustrated for Kids*. She wrote about numerous sports for the magazine and contributed to several *SI Kids* books. She lives in New Jersey with her husband.